A Life Left Unlived

In the fridge sat my dreams, quite stale,
I once planned to bake, but I just told a tale.
The cookies I planned to make all fell flat,
Now they're just a memory, like my cat's old hat.

I had a list of things I swore I'd start,
Like learning banjo or painting a dart.
But Netflix called, and I was entranced,
Now I juggle the remote, not my life, it seems chanced.

I dreamt of a road trip, the wind in my hair,
But I've been to the couch; oh, it's a fine chair.
The open road beckons with laughter and cheer,
But snacks at my side are the only ones near.

At parties, I'd boast of adventures to come,
While secretly munching on popcorn and gum.
I could have been famous, or so I would say,
While life passed me by in an all-you-can-stay.

In my mind, I'm daring, a hero of sorts,
But my sword's just a vacuum in laundry report.
I'd planned to be bold and go chase the night,
Instead, I'm just laughing with milk and a bite.

The Night We Never Spoke

We danced like fools beneath the moon,
But words got lost, too late to croon.
I tripped on thoughts I planned to share,
And laughed instead, to hide my care.

Your gaze was sharp, like cheese gone old,
While I just fumbled, feeling bold.
We laughed so much, yet silence stayed,
While dreams of chatting softly frayed.

Crumpled Letters in the Dark

The letters piled, like laundry mess,
Each folded dream held nothing less.
I wrote a note, but lost the pen,
Then turned around to laugh again.

You read my mind from miles away,
Or thought I'd call you, just to play.
The ink was smudged, but we both knew,
No message sent would ever do.

The Melody of Things Left Unsaid

A tune played softly in the air,
With lyrics lost upon a dare.
We hummed along to silence fine,
While missing beats, what a decline!

Your smile declared, my heart ached strong,
Yet still, we hummed our secret song.
In giggles wrapped, our words not found,
The melody left us both spellbound.

Requiem for a Distant Dream

A dream flew high, but we stood still,
With giggles masked, as time did spill.
We plotted plans with no voice found,
And laughed so hard, we fell to ground.

The clock ticked loud, yet we stayed meek,
Each silent laugh felt like a peak.
For words unsaid in jest we bore,
Our distant dreams forgot the score.

The Space Between Us

You said I'd call, but here we are,
My phone's on silent, you're still afar.
We laugh about cats, ignoring our fight,
And here's a joke about my poor sight.

I thought you'd show up with pizza in hand,
But now I'm left with a half-baked plan.
Your laugh's still ringing, my heart's on pause,
With every punchline, I feel the flaws.

Unseen Threads of Memory

Remember that time we danced in the rain?
Your shoes were ruined, but we felt no pain.
I told you a secret, but then forgot,
Now you think I'm the king of all thought.

You wore that hat like a crown of a fool,
While I tried to keep all the smiles in a pool.
We dodged all the raindrops, avoiding the drench,
Yet here we are, both still in a clench.

Undercurrents of Distant Wishes

A wish on a star, I tossed it your way,
It missed the target, and went astray.
You texted me later, all funny and bright,
Said, "Where's my star? You owe me tonight!"

With maps and compasses, we search high and low,
My directions are awful, just thought you should know.
To find what we dreamt, I'd need quite the guide,
But who needs a map with our hearts open wide?

Shadows Cast by the Past

In the attic of memories, ghosts play around,
We're laughing at shadows and old cardboard ground.
Those polaroids tell tales that age like fine wine,
While regret's just a punchline we weave with a twine.

You jested about my forgotten sock stash,
While we dodged all the friends you made out of cash.
The jokes on us, with a light-hearted cheer,
As we're stuck in a time warp, both laughing at fear.

Dreams That Slipped Away

I dreamed of being a rocket,
But tripped over my own socks.
The stars felt closer than my dreams,
Stuck here counting the clocks.

My plans to swim with the dolphins,
Morphed into brunch with my cat.
She looked at me, unimpressed,
While I debated that hat.

I once thought I'd be a chef,
Now I burn toast every night.
My soufflé dreams hit the floor,
Like crumbs, a sorry sight.

But laughter fills this space,
More comfort than regret.
I'll whip up plans tomorrow,
Just wait until I reset!

The Pain of Not Starting

I bought the paints, bright and bold,
To capture sunsets in style.
Now they sit, untouched, forlorn,
Collecting dust for a while.

The gym was my second home,
Until I signed up and then paused.
My plans for muscles and strength,
With snacks, my days were caused.

I had a book tucked tight in hand,
To write my life's great tale.
But here I sit with blank pages,
While my ideas grow stale.

Yet every laugh is a step,
To wash the fears away.
I'll find my groove, maybe not today,
But someday, come what may!

Labyrinths of Longing

I mapped a route to happiness,
With roads paved in candy canes.
But instead, I took a left,
And ended up in cloudy rains.

I dreamt of paths to stardom,
But found myself in a queue.
While I waited, thoughts got fuzzy,
Should've had a plan or two.

Each twist and turn led astray,
Chasing after an old train.
Now I'm just here with laughter,
Reflecting on the mundane.

But in this maze, I still dance,
With giggles that lead the way.
I'll find the exit eventually,
Or at least, a good café!

The Bitter Edge of Nostalgia

I used to be a dancer,
With dreams of dazzling the crowd.
Now I trip on my own feet,
And clap for my grace, quite loud.

I longed for days of old magic,
When life sparkled like a show.
Now it's more like sparkles in dust,
But who knew nostalgia could glow?

I gather memories like trophies,
Each mishap lined on a shelf.
Yet I giggle at my blunders,
Who needs pride when you've got self?

So here's to all the moments missed,
With laughter, a little jest.
For in every slip and fall,
I find joy's a funny guest!

When Memories Resurface

I once forgot my best friend's name,
But it was the dog that stole the fame.
In a crowd we laughed till we turned blue,
Yet here I am, it still feels askew.

At the reunion, chaos did unfold,
With awkward smiles, the tales grew old.
Why did I wear that bright pink tie?
A fashion disaster, oh me, oh my!

Time's Silent Witness

Tick tock went the clock, oh what a race,
I meant to call, but I lost my place.
When life hands you lemons, make lemonade,
But I forgot the sugar, and now I'm dismayed.

The years flew by like a sneeze on the breeze,
Missing chances like socks lost in a tease.
A smile here, a cringe there, all in good fun,
I'll keep on laughing, 'til the day is done.

A Journey of Half-Told Tales

I told a joke that fell quite flat,
My friend just stared like a puzzled cat.
The punchline danced right out of my head,
Now we're both stuck wishing I'd fled.

Embarrassment wrapped me like a warm shawl,
As I fumbled the chance to stand tall.
But hey, at least we've got good food,
To drown my fears in a pile of good mood.

The Mask We Wear

Under my grin, a secret does loom,
Like a balloon that's meant to go boom.
I tried to be cool, but I tripped on my shoe,
And now my pride is as red as my stew.

With every mask, a story to share,
All the blunders and laughs hide in there.
We're all just clowns in this grand charade,
Waving our flags of the mess we've made.

Remnants of a Faded Path

A forgotten sock beneath the bed,
Whispers tales of a long-lost thread.
The milk that soured in the fridge's light,
Laughs at the dreams of a morning bright.

A half-eaten cake, it's still on the shelf,
Resigned to think it's a treat for oneself.
A jigsaw puzzle with pieces astray,
Reminds of fun times that faded away.

The coffee cup stained from yesterday's brew,
Once held ambitions of something new.
Old grocery lists with doodles abound,
Charted paths to things never found.

A Tapestry of What Remains

Threads of laughter hang in the air,
Selfies taken, now a lost pair.
A forgotten game, its pieces askew,
Each loss a giggle, just look where we flew.

Recipes stashed in a drawer so deep,
Mixing up moments that make us weep.
The shoes on the porch with stories they know,
Of plans to dance but none made the show.

A mismatched set of old silverware,
Used for dining on casual flare.
Leftover wishes in takeout boxes,
Left to wonder where time now foxes.

Shattered Hopes

An old bicycle with a flat tire dream,
Once raced towards futures, now nothing but steam.
A worn-out board game, too tired to win,
Still offers laughs, and where we've been.

Faded shoes left by the door,
Promised paths not trodden before.
The last piece of pizza that no one will eat,
Shares the burden of defeat, oh so sweet.

A clock that ticks with a comical chime,
Reminds us we're stuck in the wrong kind of time.
A half-hearted letter, never sent out,
Giggles await that we forgot to shout.

The Space Between Moments

Between the tick and the tock of the clock,
Are all the words I forgot to unlock.
A comic strip with no punchline in sight,
Leaves us chuckling till late in the night.

The socks that don't match are now cherished friends,
Holding secrets that one never sends.
A spoonful of chaos in a cereal bowl,
Stirs unfulfilled wishes and makes my heart whole.

A crumpled receipt from a diner long gone,
Holds all the memories we still lean upon.
And the ice cream left melting in the sun's glow,
Reminds me of feelings that just refuse to go.

The Burden of Unseen Sorrows

In the garden of missed chances,
Weeds bloom where laughs once grew.
I tripped on my own excuses,
Now my plants have feelings too.

Each petal holds a secret wish,
That I could find the courage, alas!
But here I am, with just a fish,
Who also feels quite green—what a class!

The neighbor's cat gives me judgment,
As I grumble with my sad sack.
It's a feline weeping ballad,
While I plot my next snack attack.

So I water my dodgeball heart,
Watch it grow with dialing regret.
Can I write these notes in a cart?
At least my soil is fresh and wet.

Silent Footsteps on Tattered Roads

My shoes squeak louder than my silence,
Each step a chuckle in disguise.
Worms pass by with a knowing glance,
Wondering just how low I'll rise.

Maps crumple in my back pocket,
Lost paths scribbled like my hopes.
Did I take the wrong exit?
Or did I forget my anti-mopes?

Whispers float through the airways,
Like fog on a cloudy day.
Do I regret the ice cream sprinkles?
Only when life leads me astray.

Yet here I am, on my jolly trek,
Dodging cars, not regretting pies.
A life of laughter hides my wreck,
While squirrels laugh at my futile tries.

Paths Not Taken

A fork in the road, my lost chance,
I took the left, my heart did prance.
Right must be silent, never swayed,
While snacks called me, my soul displayed.

The choice of pizza over salad,
It's a battle even a fool will claim.
With each slice, the shadows rattled,
And I'm still not quite sure who's to blame.

The road to fitness waved goodbye,
As I squatted on a couch of dreams.
In my head, I'm a fitness guy,
But here in reality, pizza streams.

I peer back at paths I could've tried,
But laughter fills the air like love.
I'll blame the universe for my ride,
And just hope my stretchy pants fit, enough!

Guilt Wrapped in Stillness

In this blanket of crisp denials,
I'm wrapped up snug with all my snacks.
Didn't pay the bill, there's no trial,
But the sour cream has my backtracks.

Hiding guilt's a full-time job,
With chips and dips on the side.
A dance-off with my potato blob,
In a channel of snacks, I can hide!

While friends tell tales of epic miles,
I nod but dream of buttery rolls.
They talk of guilt, I think of styles,
As my heart sings of cheesy goals.

In every crunch, a ghost appears,
Whispering phrases I shan't repeat.
But laughter drowns out all my fears,
With flowing guac and danceable beats.

Unraveled Threads of Connection

We had a plan, oh what a joke,
A dance so clumsy, we both tripped folk.
You said you'd call, I missed your cue,
Now here we are, in a game of 'who's who.'

I bought the cake, you brought the flan,
Thought we could feast, but lost the ban.
While you were dancin', I spilled the punch,
Laughter erupted, but now I just munch.

Messages linger like old socks in drawers,
Should I text you now or just ignore yours?
A friendship on hold, like an unplayed tune,
Maybe next time? Or is that too soon?

Yet still, we giggle, a laugh or a sigh,
In this wacky world, we let moments fly.
For every oops, there's a quirky delight,
Unraveled threads weave a bond just right.

The Weight of Yesterday

I wore the shoes of yesterday's blunder,
Tripped over truths like a ship in thunder.
You raised an eyebrow, I fumbled the joke,
Oops! That awkward silence felt like a cloak.

Eggs were scrambled, plans all askew,
You said 8 a.m., but I thought 2!
Texting my fault, while you just rolled eyes,
We laughed at the chaos, beneath cloudy skies.

In the fridge lies the cake from last fall,
Half-eaten dreams stuck to the wall.
You said, 'Next time, let's order some pie!'
But here we are, the unbaked reply.

Yet somehow, it all turns to gold,
In these funny tales, our memories unfold.
Like balloons that float but never quite land,
The weight of yesterday slips from my hand.

Silent Cries for Resolution

I texted 'hello' but didn't hit send,
Worried you'd ask if we're still friends.
Instead of conflict, we laugh at the plight,
While awkward silence fills the room with light.

You showed up late with popcorn and cheese,
We laughed at the moments, and time seemed to freeze.
Each awkward silence sang louder than words,
Like a room full of frogs, leaping in herds.

Coffee mugs clinked, the steam rose like dreams,
Yet unvoiced thoughts danced like mischievous beams.
'What's next?' you asked, as you gave me a grin,
I shrugged while my heart did a little spin.

In these funny moments, the heart finds a path,
As we navigate chaos, oh, how we laugh!
With silent cries trapped in echoes we share,
Resolution can wait till we've learned how to dare.

Unmarked Graves of Moments Missed

Dancing around like clowns at the fair,
We dropped the pie, oh, the sweet despair.
You said, 'Next time, let's not be a mess,'
But oh, the laughter, who needs to confess?

Forgotten dates like socks under beds,
Spilling our secrets but losing our heads.
The stories we tell become fables of fun,
Who knew regrets could make us so spun?

Each tick of the clock laughs at our plight,
How we juggle our dreams in the fading light.
You forgot the napkins, I forgot the rhyme,
But isn't it splendid to waste all this time?

So here's to the moments, unmarked and bizarre,
We laugh at the past, like a shooting star.
For every missed chance, there's a giggle or two,
In this dance of life, I'll always choose you.

Lingering in the Aftermath

I dropped the ball, again, you see,
Like juggling ice cream, just for me.
Forgot the date, or did I scheme?
Now I'm lost in a half-baked dream.

The socks I lost, they haunt my mind,
In every corner, they're hard to find.
If only I had labeled them right,
Now they're dancing in the moonlight.

Chasing thoughts like runaway cats,
They slip through my fingers, like silly hats.
I laugh as I tumble, what a delight,
In a mess of my own making, oh what a sight!

So here's to the blunders we can't forget,
With chuckles and giggles, no need to fret.
For in the chaos, there's always a wink,
Just grab a snack and don't overthink!

Nods to Yesterday

I waved to the past with a crumpled smile,
Wishing I'd known, if just for a while.
An old friend's name slips from my lips,
As I ponder if that's how time drips.

Each 'oops' is a badge, don't you see?
Like wearing mismatched socks, it's just me.
In the clutter of choices, I trip and fall,
Yet I laugh at the echoes, that's the best of all.

Did I really eat that cake and think,
"I'll work it off," as I sip and blink?
The crumbs of yesterday stick like glue,
But maybe that's just what we do.

So let's toast to moments that went awry,
To the giggling regrets that make us sigh.
With friends around, we'll toast and cheer,
For life's silly dances, a merry smear!

Between Breath and Thought

A hiccup of laughter, the pause inside,
Where thoughts of the past want to run and hide.
Did I really send that text with a grin?
Now I'm stuck wondering what shape I'm in.

The socks beneath the bed, a secret lair,
And the stories they tell, oh, if they dare!
Each stitch holds a giggle, a tale or two,
Of moments forgotten that feel so askew.

Did I say what I meant or just blurt out noise?
In the carnival of life, there's no one to toys.
Yet, echoes of laughter dance in my head,
As I sit with my cake and my bittersweet bread.

So here's to the whimsy, the wild and the whack,
To the things we've lost, and the moments we pack.
With every chuckle, we lighten the load,
In the grand game of living, we dance down the road!

Veils of the Untold

Behind every giggle, there's a tale undone,
Like a juggler in slippers, just having fun.
I swore I'd call back, yet my phone went cold,
Chasing after words, my doubts unfold.

Forgotten plans dance in the back of my brain,
Where friendships go wandering, trying to gain.
Did I really bail on that taco night meal?
Now my stomach's grumbling, oh, the appeal!

In the land of the 'what ifs' and 'oh, know thy fate',
I giggle at puns that may not translate.
Each laugh is a bridge, a signpost of glee,
As I wander through memories, just being me.

So let's raise our glasses to lessons in jest,
For each silly moment becomes one of the best.
In the tapestry woven of laughter and sighs,
We find the delight hidden deep in our eyes!

The Sound of Holding Back

In a room of awkward silence,
Laughter dances like a ghost.
We sip on soda, eyes downcast,
Cracking jokes, but it feels like toast.

Whispers of thoughts float by,
Like balloons tied to a tree.
We joke about the things we held,
But no one dares to set them free.

My tongue's a trampoline,
Bouncing words that don't quite land.
We all laugh, but it's a tune,
That only we can understand.

We shuffle feelings like cards,
Hiding aces up our sleeves.
With each laugh, a truth departs,
But nobody really believes.

An Empty Chair at the Table

The chair sits there, uninvited,
A witness to the awkward feast.
We toast to friends who've drifted,
Yet the chair's the one partied least.

I swear it's plotting some mischief,
With crumbs and spills in its favor.
"Fill me up!" it silently pleads,
But we just laugh and do a favor.

Conversations bounce off its wood,
Like ping pong balls gone astray.
It rolls its eyes in quiet grief,
While we joke about yesterday.

It's the ghost of good times gone,
With stories stuck in its seams.
Each joke a wish that stings with love,
That stays unspoken in our dreams.

The Colors of Longing

If longing were a paint, I'd say,
I'd splash it on walls bold and bright.
Each hue a laugh, a hint of truth,
A canvas full of banter's light.

Blue of the days I meant to call,
Green for the plans that slipped away.
A rainbow of wishes, mingled ties,
Fading slowly to shades of gray.

Every stroke's a chance we missed,
Fun times wrapped in silent hue.
We giggle at the wrong turns made,
But a smile won't paint it true.

In this gallery of what-ifs,
We laugh at the absurd parade.
Yet here we are, still side by side,
With colors of longing unmade.

Fading Footprints

In sand's embrace, our footprints dance,
But waves of time wash them away.
We stride on paths of laughter bright,
Yet twinge for words we didn't say.

Each step a chuckle, soft and sly,
Yet deeper thoughts are swept from view.
We race the tide, avoid the truth,
Making splashy jokes, all askew.

The shore's our stage, but oh, so grand,
Fading echoes sing our refrain.
"Remember when?" we laugh and jest,
But a sigh rolls in like gentle rain.

With every wave, a heartbeat misses,
The sand holds secrets, light as air.
We laugh until the night falls deep,
Leaving fading footprints, unaware.

In the Stillness, I Weep

In silence, I ponder, what a silly mess,
My socks still unmatched, oh, what a distress.
The toast burnt to ashes, I just can't believe,
Should've marked my calendar, or at least worn my
sleeve.

Thoughts sneak like ninjas, they dance in my head,
Should've called my mom, but I chose Netflix instead.
Laughter chokes me, like coffee down the wrong pipe,
These thoughts—oh, what antics—like an old grapevine
type.

The cat gives me judgment, as I ponder my fate,
Did I forget my friend's birthday, or just procrastinate?
Regret, like a jester, pulls a prank from the past,
I'll nail it next time, I'll make the card last!

So here I sit chuckling, a smirk on my face,
These silly little regrets—they've turned into grace.
With laughter my armor, I rise from the ground,
In the silence of jest, my calmness is found.

Fragments of the Heart Untold

Oh, peeking at memories through a silly old lens,
Like mismatched clipart, or my odd collection of pens.
I meant to apologize, but my pride deemed it tough,
So I sent them a meme instead—was that good enough?

Dancing around feelings like ants on a hill,
Forgotten milestones tangled up, oh, what a thrill!
I wore socks with sandals, played my quirky part,
And laughed at the courage to hide my own heart.

I made promises sweet, like candy-coated lies,
But who'd have known they'd be snuck off in disguise?
Like cupcakes without frosting, they fizzle and fade,
A sprinkle of humor's a fine way to trade.

So here's to the fragments, the giggles we hide,
In the scrapbook of life, let's enjoy the wild ride.
I'll toast to those moments, hold out my cup,
And laugh with the echoes, won't ever give up.

The Ghosts We Leave Behind

In the attic of conscience, where old echoes dwell,
The ghosts of my choices invite me to yell.
They waltz through my dreams, wearing outdated clothes,

Whispering tales of mishaps and woe in prose.

I tripped on a truth, fell flat on my face,
Told a joke at the party, was that really my place?
The punchline was flying, but my timing was off,
Now it haunts my mornings, like the coffee I scoff.

The avatars of blunders keep popping around,
With their ghostly giggles, they follow my sound.
"Remember that time?" they tease with delight,
In shadows, we chuckle, until late in the night.

Each blush and each cringe, a case of the shivers,
They float through my mind like my old teenage quivers.
But laughter, sweet laughter, deflates all the fright,
With humor, I seal them, in the soft gentle light.

Constellations of Regret

Staring at stardust, the cosmos awakes,
Each twinkle a moment, oh, the choices it makes.
I'd mapped out the heavens, designed a grand scheme,
But now, look at me—lost in my ice cream dream!

I scribbled my plans on the back of a napkin,
Promised the world, but my calendar's napping.
Instead of saying 'hi', I just waved from afar,
Now my love life's a comet—yep, oh there goes that star!

A laugh through the milestones, they sparkle and giggle,
Each regret, a reminder—a wiggly wiggle.
The universe chuckles, says "Dear, don't be blue,
Your choices make starlight—this sky's just for you!"

So I'll gather my wishes, like fireflies caught,
Embrace all the blunders, hey, nothing's for naught.
With each cherished misstep, I'll dance in the night,
Constellations of laughter, my heart in their light.

Beneath the Surface of Smiles

I wore a grin, made it bright,
Underneath, oh what a sight.
Jokes flew high, laughter loud,
But my heart just felt too cowed.

Balloons and cake filled the room,
Yet my thoughts were filled with gloom.
Dancing feet and silly puns,
Hide the weight of missed-out fun.

In every toast, a secret sigh,
As I raised my glass up high.
Should've spoke, should've shared more,
Instead, I just closed that door.

So here's to laughs, a light facade,
Behind my smile, a road most flawed.
A chuckle shared, a wink or two,
But regrets, they just stick like glue.

Fragile Threads of Thought

In my mind, ideas twist and twine,
Like spaghetti on a fork so fine.
I chuckle softly, keep it light,
Yet there's silence in the night.

Witty comebacks slid away,
As I stood there, lost in play.
Should've told you how I felt,
Instead, I just stood there, knelt.

Laughter echoed, jokes exchanged,
But inside, I felt so strange.
Threads of thought, so hard to weave,
Trapped in words I couldn't leave.

Oh, the fun that we might've had,
In every moment, I felt glad.
Yet here I stand, with knots in mind,
As laughter fades, I'm left behind.

The Cost of Indecision

At the crossroads of a quirky fate,
I pondered long, deliberated late.
Choice A or B, both seem so bright,
Yet here I am, stuck in the night.

Should I wear the blue or the red?
In my mind, a battle spread.
While time ticks by like a slow mime,
I chuckle softly, wasting time.

The ice cream shop across the street,
Glistening flavors oh so sweet.
But here I stand, lost in the haze,
Indecision leads to hazy days.

So here's a toast, with whipped cream high,
To silly choices, oh me, oh my.
Next time I'll just pick and run,
Or else I might just weigh a ton!

Memories That Whisper

In a photo booth, we made silly faces,
But beneath the laughs, a heart slowly races.
Oh, the things I didn't say then,
Turned into whispers, as we met as friends.

Every shared secret, a story untold,
Wrapped in laughter, hidden in gold.
Yet in the silence, I felt the ache,
A joke to tell, a chance to take.

I remember how you danced in the rain,
While I stood wrapped in my own little pain.
Oh, how I wish I had jumped right in,
Instead, I stayed dry, a fool in sin.

So here's to laughter, as light as air,
But every giggle holds a hidden care.
For in each chuckle, a sigh may dwell,
Filling our hearts with stories to tell.

Ghosts of Choices Past

I bought a cake instead of shoes,
And now I dance in icing blues.
The frosting laughs, a jolly ghost,
Regrets taste best, I think, at most.

I skipped that call, to binge a show,
Now I can't join the friend I owe.
The popcorn whispers from the bowl,
Each kernel pops, my heart's in thrall.

Oh, broccoli, I waved goodbye,
To pizza's charm, I said, 'Oh my!'
Now veggies haunt my dreams at night,
While cheesy laughter takes its flight.

Those choices wink from shadows tall,
I laugh and cry, yet must recall,
The joy in mishaps, oh so bright,
In ghosts of choices, wrong feels right.

Shadows of What Could Have Been

I chose a cat, got hit by fate,
While dogs are cool, they just can't wait.
A feline's grace in every leap,
Yet doggy dreams, I lost some sleep.

That date I missed, to stay in bed,
Now he's a star, I just feels dread.
With popcorn shared and laughter rife,
I could have danced a different life.

My paintbrush swayed, I picked the wrong,
Instead of art, I wrote this song.
Oh, wish I'd smudged those colors bright,
Now black and white feels far too tight.

The shadows chuckle, teasing me,
With every path, a mystery.
In laughter's glow, I see them fade,
What could have been, a charade made.

The Weight of Words Unsaid

I held my tongue, a champion feat,
As friends all danced, oh what a treat.
They spun and twirled, I just sat still,
My words in chains, oh what a thrill!

When compliments were due, I balked,
Instead I sighed, and awkwardly walked.
Their smiles grew wide, and I just froze,
In heavy silence, nothing flows.

That text I wrote, but didn't send,
"Hey, let's meet up!" was my intent.
But now I'm left with this old phone,
A gadget full of words unsown.

The weight of silence, hard to bear,
Yet my ghost chuckles in mid-air.
In every missed chance, laughter's blend,
The weight of words can still transcend.

Fragments of Forgotten Dreams

I dreamed of fame, a star so bright,
But tripped on shoes, fell out of sight.
My glittering plans fell to the floor,
While laughter echoed, forevermore.

In every page, a story missed,
The plotline bends, with irony kissed.
My dreams skated off, on ice so thin,
While I, the clown, just can't win.

Those artful sketches, I left behind,
Now doodles haunt, my mind entwined.
Each scribbled line a chuckle shared,
In fragments sweet, my past declared.

Yet here I stand, with humor bold,
Embracing dreams, both shy and old.
In laughter's arms, I find my muse,
Forgotten dreams, I gladly choose.

Ink Stains on Unwritten Pages

I penned a tale, but lost the pen,
Now it's a saga of where and when.
My thoughts are wild, they jump and run,
But all that's left is just the fun.

I had a plan, a glorious scheme,
But on my couch, I fell asleep.
The words are there, I swear they tease,
With wiped-out dreams and coffee glees.

My notebook cries with all its might,
It had a party, but I missed the night.
The pen's ink spilled on empty forms,
And now it's just a muse in storms.

So here's to stories in the air,
Where wishes go but seldom dare.
I laugh at pages that never show,
Ink stains, oh where did my good ideas go?

A Heart Full of Silence

In crowded rooms, I sip my tea,
With tales unsaid, how can it be?
I crack a joke, but none will land,
My heart's a mime, not quite so grand.

I tried to flirt with a clever line,
But ended up just counting time.
My heart plays charades with all the feels,
While laughter hides the truth it steals.

A wink, a smile, I start to sway,
But words dance off and run away.
Oh, the silent clowns at my command,
Leave me jester of this empty land.

So raise a toast to what's not said,
A quiet heart inside my head.
I'll wear my laughter like a crown,
While silence giggles, upside down.

The Garden of Missed Chances

In my backyard, the weeds are high,
Missed blooms wave the day goodbye.
I planted hopes, but what a mess,
This garden needs a new address.

Miracles tucked in packets tight,
But never watered, they fell from sight.
I had a plan for roses bright,
But now it's just a joke in fright.

The veggies promised by the packet,
Are substitutes for vernal racket.
With gnomes that chuckle at my loss,
My gardening skills are at a toss.

So here I stand, a weedy throng,
With laughter echoing all night long.
My garden dreams, they let me down,
Yet still I strut in laughter's gown.

Unseen Wounds

A bruise that's hiding, all concealed,
My laughter echoes, fate revealed.
I trip on jokes that never land,
With a smile plastered, just like sand.

I grin through pain, oh what a mess,
My heart's a dancer, in distress.
Each chuckle's a band-aid, paper thin,
Masking the chaos that lurks within.

Invisible cuts in the laughter's flow,
My friends still wonder, 'Is it a show?'
I play the fool, in silken threads,
While mischief whispers what's left unsaid.

So I'll joke and jest, to keep the peace,
In a world where stitches never cease.
With unseen wounds, I twirl about,
In the carnival of laughter, I'll shout!

Conversations with Shadows

They dance in the corners of my mind,
Whispering secrets I can't quite find.
They giggle about the things I missed,
While I trip on shoes I should've kissed.

A missed call from the fridge, it roars,
'You left me alone for takeout stores!'
I laugh as the shadows pull at my sleeve,
'Can't I just enjoy my spaghetti weave?'

They tell me of dreams that took a holiday,
Cardboard cutouts that fade away.
With a wink and a nudge, they tease my frown,
'Why not wear regrets like a goofy crown?'

In this room full of silence and cheer,
My shadows remind me that I should steer.
Not all is lost in the humorous ballet,
Life's a punchline, so come out and play!

A Room Filled with Unsaid Things

This space is cluttered with what I missed,
A sock puppet that's wearing a fist.
It chirps about the words left unsaid,
While a cactus pops off with a cheeky thread.

The thoughts float like balloons stuck in the air,
One's got a grin, the other's a scare.
A soapbox of giggle that's bursting at seams,
While I sit here juggling my unhatched dreams.

A light switch flickers, it's playing coy,
As my regrets try to be the life of the joy.
'Low battery,' I sigh, 'and yet we play,'
While my thoughts box dance in a silly ballet.

Imagine a closet filled with old shoes,
Each pair tells stories of past misconstrues.
Yet the sneakers shout, 'Let's dash out and roam!'
'We'll trip on tomorrow's grand stage—our home!'

Sunsets of Forgotten Hopes

The sun dips low, dressed in gold and red,
A wardrobe of dreams that I never fed.
While clouds chuckle, saying 'Where you been?'
In a cosmic tease, they paint a grin.

Each sunset winks as if it knows,
About half-baked plans and forgotten shows.
I scratch my head at lost limelight,
While shadows twirl in a silly flight.

An umbrella of wishes abandoned in rain,
Blooms with laughter—'Let's dance through the pain!'
A fruitcake of laughter makes the world sway,
As sunset whispers, 'Tomorrow's a play!'

But here's the punchline to all of this,
I'll keep laughing as I do a head spin twist.
With each fading light comes a new chance to vibe,
In the quirky slapstick of this life we describe.

The Quiet Storm of Regret

Here's a tempest brewing in a teacup,
It's laughing and bubbling as we hiccup.
The skies are gray, but don't lose your cheer,
For even clouds enjoy a cotton candy beer.

It rumbles lightly, like a chuckle in sleep,
While I pile up bones of promises deep.
A lightning bolt's winking, saying 'Hey dude!'
Let's tango with giggles in this echoing mood.

The wind howls tales of a very odd past,
Each gust throws my thoughts out so fast.
With umbrellas of humor, let's ride out the gale,
As we dance in the rain, our boots come to bail.

So let's raise a glass to these storms that we face,
The quietest chuckles stitch up this space.
In a whirlwind of laughter, let memories sway,
For tomorrow's a joke that we'll all want to play!

In the Quiet of Our Minds

In the corner of my brain, it sits,
A joke unshared, full of hits.
I laugh alone at my own gaffes,
While you sip tea, ignoring the path.

We dance around the truth so light,
Like awkward clowns in the moonlight.
Our thoughts collide, yet smiles we fake,
Like blaming the cake for the mistake.

If only we could spill the beans,
On all the silly, crazy scenes.
We'd burst with laughter, then return,
To thoughts untold—a funny burn.

So raise a glass, let's toast tonight,
To awkward silence, oh what a sight!
We'll giggle softly, hearts in a twine,
In the quiet of our minds, so divine.

Masks of Silent Longing

Behind my grin, a circus hides,
Where clowns play tricks and laughter bides.
We wear our masks, oh what a show,
Pretending well, while feelings grow.

You cracked a joke, I didn't share,
But deep inside, there's a flair.
Like mimes in a park, we dance and sway,
Wishing for words we'll never say.

Your hidden dreams, they haunt the night,
While I toss and turn, out of sheer fright.
We laugh at shadows, and share a glance,
In this crazy game, we never dance.

So here we sit, both side by side,
With masks of longing we cannot hide.
Though humor flows, here's the twist,
Those golden words will be missed.

Echoes in the Void

In an empty room, my thoughts replay,
Echoing laughs that drift away.
A funny face, then a quirked brow,
In the void, we lost it somehow.

Tickle my heart, but don't say a thing,
We'll joke about what the silence can bring.
Like echoes bouncing off the walls,
Our laughter's trapped—oh the gall!

We flip through memories as we dine,
Each unvoiced thought becomes a line.
Perhaps the punchline was never clear,
As we sip on our unspoken beer.

Yet in this emptiness, hearts collide,
Trapped in comedy, we won't confide.
We laugh at ghosts, though they annoy,
In this echo chamber, we find some joy.

Forgotten Promises

We promised to text, but time slipped through,
Now I send memes to fake a 'hello' too.
Forgotten vows float like chicken fry,
In the bubbling oil of our goofy sighs.

A pact of giggles we failed to keep,
Like a diet plan that's gone too deep.
Yet here we sit, with sweet repartee,
As veggies we planned turn out to be brie.

Our friendship blooms behind the sighs,
Where laughter lives, and humor lies.
We tripped on memories, such silly trips,
With forgotten promises on our lips.

So here's to chaos and plans gone astray,
In this funny mess, we find our way.
With every chuckle, let's bind our schemes,
And giggle at life's forgotten dreams.

Faded Dreams

In a cupboard, my dreams lay dusted,
Like old cereal, by time rusted.
We giggle at plans that never went right,
While ghostly hopes dance in the night.

We plotted grand schemes over popcorn nights,
Yet ended up tangled in silly fights.
Each dream, a balloon, now a faint hue,
Floating away like a prank meant for you.

Yet in the fading, there's magic too,
For silly ideas still come shining through.
Like a past joke that eludes our lips,
We chuckle softly at fate's little quips.

So let's toast to dreams, both bright and bland,
In this wild party, we'll take a stand.
With laughter's sweet echo, we'll never part,
For the faded sparks still shine in our heart.

The Road Not Taken

Two paths beside the stream,
One looked sweet, the other a dream.
I took the snack route, what a treat,
Missed the views, but got ice cream!

In flip-flops I strolled, what a sight,
Lost my map, can't remember right.
Friends laugh hard at my dumb plight,
I'm chilling solo, feeling light.

Should I've worn shoes? Maybe so,
But who knew mud was part of the show?
Years later I still trip below,
In life's great race, I'm slow and low!

So here I strut, a prince of fun,
Dancing on paths where I come undone.
Regrets? Nah, just look at me run,
With joy, my friend, I've already won!

Futile Hopes Adrift

I tossed a coin in a wishing well,
Hoping for fortune, what the hell?
Instead of gold, I heard a yell,
Turns out it's just an old seashell!

I planned a trip, grand and wide,
Pack my bags with dreams inside.
But Netflix calls, I just can't hide,
So here I lie, the couch my guide.

Thought I'd dance under the moonlight,
But fell asleep before the night.
Regret? Nah, the dream was bright,
Next year I swear, I'll take that flight!

Futile hopes, like bubbles burst,
But who needs fancy, when snacks are first?
I'll sip my soda, quench my thirst,
In hilarious blunders, I'm immersed!

Silent Echoes

In the closet, secrets rest,
Forgotten shoes, I must confess.
A pair I wore to a silly fest,
But now they whisper of my bad jest.

Voices linger in my head,
Choices made, paths that I dread.
Like that party where I misread,
And danced like jelly, now I'm fed!

Echoes laugh at my wild moves,
Chasing dreams, like rubber grooves.
The memories twist, and still it proves,
That humor thrives, as panic soothes.

So I embrace each awkward fumble,
With every stumble, I laugh and tumble.
In silent echoes, I refuse to grumble,
For in this life, we all must jumble!

Whispers of the Heart

I wrote a love note, sweet and bold,
But it slipped away, oh behold!
Now birds keep singing stories untold,
And I'm left wondering about the gold.

Wished to confess my crush's name,
But chicken out, what a shame!
Now my heart's playing a silly game,
Whispers linger, but who's to blame?

In dreams, we frolic, hand in hand,
But then reality's a different land.
I trip on words I never planned,
With every giggle, it feels so grand.

So here's to secrets, light as air,
To every hope, to every care.
Life's a sitcom, we're all laid bare,
In whispers of the heart, there's laughter to share!

When Time Stands Still

Tick-tock, the clock won't budge,
A dance with time, what a grudge!
I missed that chance for a quick wink,
Staring at my drink, I start to think.

Moments lost, like socks in a dryer,
Should've danced, not just admired.
I'd made a joke, but it was too late,
Now I'm the punchline—oh, isn't fate great?

The laughter fades, but I've got my seat,
At the comedy club of life, can't take defeat.
I'll make new friends, maybe stick to the plan,
But first, let's talk about that one awkward man!

So here I sit, with soft drinks in hand,
Regretting nothing—just trying to stand.
When time stands still, I sip and I grin,
Who knows what future laughs I might win?

Buried Hopes and Silent Cries

In a garden where dreams go to rest,
I planted my wishes, but I lost the quest.
Weeds grow tall where my laughter once bloomed,
Now I just chuckle, feeling doomed.

"Oh, I'll get to it!" I'd swear on the moon,
But that mission is lost, like an old favorite tune.
Tomorrow I'll conquer, just wait and you'll see,
But tomorrow keeps laughing—what's wrong with me?

Overdue tickets for a life on the shelf,
A movie of dreams, I edited myself.
The plot twists are funny, but unplanned, oh dear!
I'm the leading lady of my comedy sphere.

Laughter echoes where my hopes used to thrive,
I joke about life, just to feel alive.
So here's to the buried, let's dig and unearth,
For buried hopes can sprout laughter, for what it's worth.

Dreams Left on the Shelf

Once I had dreams like books on a shelf,
So dusty and quiet, I forgot to delve.
They whispered, "Read us!" but I was too busy,
Playing it safe, oh so very dizzy.

The chapters are wild, the plots quite absurd,
In one, I'm a ninja; in another, a bird.
But here I sit, not even a peep,
Imagination's playground now feels like deep sleep.

I laugh at the stories that gather such moss,
Each untold tale, a tiny loss.
A hero I'd be, if only I'd try,
But I binge watch reruns as the moments fly by.

So let's dust off these dreams, give them a chance,
Maybe they'll twirl, and lead me to dance.
For life's just a script, and I'm the author supreme,
Let's turn the page and wake up from this dream.

The Language of Lost Chances

Talking in circles, I trip on my words,
Every missed call, a flock of lost birds.
I wrote a love note but slipped it away,
Now I just chuckle at my silent display.

Conversations halted, like a train gone off track,
Each awkward pause feels like a friendly smack.
Should I have said more, or just played the fool?
I'm the star of my show, and oh—what a duel!

Chances float by like balloons in the breeze,
I'll chase them tomorrow, if you'd just say please.
But first, let's eat snacks and pretend that we care,
Who needs romance when you've got chips to share?

So here's to the words that fell through the cracks,
I'll gather the remnants, and laugh at the facts.
The language of losing might sometimes seem grim,
But humor's the light on a faded out whim.

The Language of Silence

In a room where words forgot to dance,
A cat named Whiskers took a chance.
He said nothing but gave a stare,
Which spoke volumes, quite unfair!

His owner sighed, with coffee in hand,
Pondering dreams, just like a band.
But Whiskers napped instead of prancing,
While the world outside kept advancing.

Once upon a time, plans on a whim,
To Paris! To dine! But dreams were slim.
Instead, they feasted on instant meals,
With sitcoms echoing their squeals.

But laughter bubbled up so bright,
In comfy sweats, they found delight.
A world outside, but who would roam?
When couch and chips felt just like home.

Balloons floated high, plans tangled like strings,
But life's little quirks have all sorts of wings.
Like socks unmatched, drifting through air,
While wishes roam wild without a care.

In the silence, unclaimed joys bloom,
With jokes and chuckles that fill the room.
So here's to moments that slipped away,
But gave us laughter, come what may!

Pockets Full of Wishes

In pockets deep, where dreams reside,
Fell through the cracks, like plans misplaced.
A snow globe wedding, or so they claimed,
But inner kid sighed, 'Guess I'm too tame!'

They strolled along, tossed coins with flair,
Hoping for magic, but nothing was there.
Yet giggles erupted in spontaneous sprees,
As rain kissed the pavement, bringing them glee.

With a sandwich jammed, she took a big bite,
Planning a hike, but lunch felt just right.
The mountains called out, "Are you there yet?"
While the couch and a show roasted popcorn's set.

Dancing with socks that had gone on strike,
The mischief of life, it's all just alike.
For unpicked choices just made them smile,
As seasons passed by, each quirky mile.

So here's to the pockets all filled to the brim,
With plans gone awry, still happy and dim.
Laughter is currency worth more than gold,
With every odd turn, more stories unfold.

Echoes of Lost Possibilities

In a closet of dreams, dust bunnies creak,
Memories sealed, where nobody speaks.
An empty stage, the curtain still drawn,
With echoes of 'what if' teetering on.

Battles of voices, they play hide and seek,
In a world full of chatter, they feel so bleak.
Yet inside a giggle lurks out of sight,
Painting the walls with colors so bright.

Days drift along, like ships in the breeze,
While pondering choices under tall trees.
"Should I have danced?" they think with a frown,
As squirrels put on quite the show in the town!

While coffee turned cold in the whirlwind of life,
And the dog snored loudly, a creature of strife.
Regrets float like feathers, light as they fall,
But laughter finds space in the echoes of all.

In the end, who cares 'bout plans that went wrong?
In a melody sweet, they've found where they belong.
So here's to the echoes that jingle and jive,
For in funny mishaps, dreams still survive!

Hidden in the Silence

Beneath the whispers of a quiet room,
Where secrets piled high like old forgotten gloom.
The clock ticked loudly, counting the air,
While laughter danced softly, oblivious to care.

With a plate piled high but appetite shy,
"To eat or not to eat?" they pondered and sighed.
Yet eyes twinkled bright, 'What's next on the list?'
As they swirled into dreams with a giggly twist.

In corners of silence, the chuckles did bloom,
Tickling fancy amid the mundane room.
They debated on who would sing loudly two,
While the cat rolled over, like "What's wrong with you?"

Life's little whispers turned grand into small,
With socks piled high, that adorned the hall.
Regrets half forgotten, mix laughter with cheer,
In the quietest moments, their joy's crystal clear.

So lift up your voice, let silence unfold,
In a canvas of mishaps, more stories are told.
With every laugh shared, the shadows did play,
And hidden in silence, memories still sway.

Labyrinth of Lost Moments

I chased my dreams like a cat in a tree,
Only to find a squirrel's mockery.
Each step a twist, a turn, a laugh,
In this maze of mishaps, I'm the epitaph.

Forgot to confess my crush on a pie,
Lemon meringue winked, oh my, oh my!
I skipped my chance, the moment flew,
And now I'm left feeling like a raw stew.

I lost my keys while searching for fun,
They hid in the sofa, oh what a pun!
Now seeking joy seems a jester's game,
In this labyrinth, just me and my shame.

Regretting those days when I just said, "Maybe,"
Filled with "what ifs," oh, how they can be!
Each giggle a ghost of what I should've said,
While I munch on the crumbs of the path I tread.

Beneath a Silence Heavy with Meaning

In the stillness, where laughter should play,
I clutched my words, let them slip away.
Like balloons at a party, they faded from sight,
Now I'm just a mime in this silent plight.

A sundae ice cream, it dripped on my shoes,
I watched my sweet dreams turn into bad news.
A scoop of regret, topped with a cherry,
Turned sticky and sad, it felt rather merry.

The whispers I lost to a loud, crowded room,
While my heart danced alone, it met its own gloom.
I raised my glass, but alone at the bar,
My toast to the silence felt somewhere bizarre.

Each chuckle not shared now haunts me like ghosts,
In this quiet confusion, I'm missing my hosts.
But who's to say what the silence confides?
Maybe it's laughter that everyone hides!

A Tapestry of Missed Connections

Knots of fate woven in colors so bright,
Yet I tangled my strings in a comical fight.
A dance without steps, I stepped on my toes,
Weaving mishaps, where the chaos only grows.

In the café of life, I missed the last call,
Spilled coffee on dreams, oh, how could I fall?
With every sip taken, my heart tugged at strings,
But the order I placed went to chickens with wings.

A tap on the shoulder, I turned but too late,
The laughter still echoes, a quirky fate.
I wave at the memories, they wave back a grin,
In this tapestry woven, where the wild truths begin.

Each thread tells a tale of missed chances and puns,
Embroidered in laughter, where everyone runs.
But fear not the laughter; it's a friend of our past,
In this tapestry grand, let's embrace it at last.

Reflections in a Broken Mirror

Gazing at shards of a long-lost regret,
Each piece a story, a joke not quite set.
I wink at my likeness, it laughs right back,
In this broken reflection, I avoid the crack.

A million faces, not one hits the mark,
I'm just a clown with a well-placed quark.
Juggling regrets, the punchline's my fate,
Still I slip on the banana, it's all up for debate.

With every glance, I see smiles that should've been,
But they dance in the ether, a ghostly sheen.
Laughter that echoes in shadows of glass,
Time's a comedian, letting moments just pass.

So here's to the mischief, the jests left behind,
In this broken mirror, true humor I find.
Each crack tells a tale of the joy and the jest,
Even in fragments, we must wish for the best.

Cycles of Reflection

I looked at my shoes, they stared back at me,
Dancing with dust, that's my legacy.
The past wears a grin, as it teases my mind,
But my future's a mess, and it's one of a kind.

A muffin I dropped, it rolled down the street,
A metaphor, yes, for my own two left feet.
Each time I think back, I laugh then I frown,
For every small choice, I've dropped my own crown.

The echoes of choices flit here and there,
Like socks in a dryer that vanish in air.
But laughter can help, to lighten the load,
While I trip on this path, of my own comical road.

So let's toast to the blunders that brought us to glee,
With a laugh and a wink, let's pass on the plea.
For life's just a jest, and the jester's our role,
We'll juggle our worries, and just take a stroll.

Foresight Forged in Silence

With a wink and a nod, I forged a great plan,
To avoid all the mess, yes, an admirable man.
But silence rarely whispers sweet strategies clear,
And I fumbled like spaghetti, much to my own fear.

The signs were all there, I just didn't see,
Like a dog with no leash, running wild and free.
Yet hindsight's a pirate, laughs loud in the night,
As I trip on the tales that I thought I made right.

Invitations were sent, but I missed every clue,
Like fresh-baked cookies, that I never could chew.
I watched from the shadows, with popcorn in hand,
As my life turned to sitcom, oh isn't it grand?

So cheers to the quiet that led me astray,
For life's little jokes keep the gloom far away.
I'll embrace every stumble, and wear it with pride,
In this circus called life, as I slip and I slide.

The Heart's Heavy Atlas

My heart wears a map, drawn with crayons so bold,
Filled with paths I once traveled, some wondrous, some
cold.
Each line's a reminder of the routes I took fast,
Yet now as I ponder, I just laugh at the past.

There's a bridge I once built, it's now crammed with
weeds,
Built on dreams half-formed, and last-minute needs.
I fall in the gaps, when I slip on my thought,
But the laughter that bubbles brings joy to the lot.

Each valley of sorrow, each mountain of woe,
Hold stories of silence, where I dare not go.
But through every misstep, there's wiggles and spunk,
For my heart's heavy atlas is fit for a funk.

So here's to the bumps, and the lumpy old roads,
To the laughter and silliness, lightening loads.
I'll sketch new adventures, with crayons on hand,
As I giggle and wander through this comedic land.

Lost in the Spaces Between

In the pauses of chatter, I find laughter's glow,
Like a tumbleweed rolling, with nowhere to go.
I mimic the moments, but trip on the grace,
As I dance with unsaid words in this goofy space.

Each sigh is a punchline that gets lost at the door,
While my brain does a jig to a tune I ignore.
Flashing back to whispers, I never quite caught,
Like a sock in the wash that I've cherished a lot.

The pauses grow heavier, and jokes start to swell,
Like a cat with a furball, I'm trapped in this shell.
Yet in every odd silence, a giggle will creep,
As I embrace every quirk that's too silly to keep.

So here's to the gaps where my humor runs wild,
To the secrets unshared that delay me, beguiled.
I'll prance through the spaces, like a clown with a dream,
Finding joy in the laughter, or so it would seem.

Roads Untaken

I walked a path, so bright and clear,
But chose instead that awful pier.
The fish were biting, or so they said,
Instead I tripped, and fell on my head.

Oh, what was that like? A laugh in disguise,
A sunken treasure, oh what a surprise!
The road not taken brought giggles and glee,
But what if the fish were just waiting for me?

I left my shoes, and sometimes my pride,
But those silly moments, I'll not try to hide.
Each road untraveled, a story to tell,
With extra pounds lost, if only I fell!

So raise a toast, to paths gone astray,
To the roads untaken, and laughs on display!
With every wrong turn, a chuckle we find,
In every mistake, the best stories unwind.

Faces of My Past

I met an old friend, he cried, and I laughed,
His hair was a forest, my, what a draft!
He told me of dreams, and girls he adored,
I nodded and chuckled, my memories floored.

We reminisced about the days gone by,
The awkward kisses, the silly goodbye.
Faces change slowly, like cheese in the sun,
But every wild laugh still brings out the fun.

Oh, that time in a dance, tripped over a shoe,
I landed on stage with a great view, it's true!
His face turned tomato, I snorted, I wheezed,
In the annals of laughter, I was wholly pleased.

So raise your glass high, to faces we knew,
To memories packed, like an old worn shoe.
Each chuckle a knot on the heart's tapestry,
Binding us together, in joyful memory!

The Price of Silence

A secret I kept, for a long, long while,
It started as hush, but ended in guile.
I whispered too softly, a sneeze changed the tone,
Now my goldfish knows more than my phone.

The price of silence, oh what a cost!
I missed out on parties, and fun that I lost.
While I munched on chips, and crunched every vow,
My friends won at bingo, they're great at the how.

A chuckle, a wink, a giggle so bold,
Could've saved me from winds, both chilly and cold.
But here I sit, with my potato chips,
Wondering why my insecurity trips.

Now I shout from rooftops, my heart all laid bare,
The price of silence? A coat I must wear.
But with every loud cheer, I balance the score,
For every sad hiccup, there's laughter galore!

Memories Behind Closed Doors

Behind closed doors, secrets unfold,
Like a cat in a hat, but a sight to behold!
I tiptoed so softly, with snacks in my hand,
To find grandma's hidden, mysterious band.

They played on old radios, off-key and sweet,
A symphony made of fudge and stale beet.
My uncles all danced, with choreography strange,
While I burst out laughing, my cheeks in exchange.

Those moments tucked tight, like cookies in jars,
Each giggle a treasure, no need for old stars.
I peek and I ponder, what else has been missed?
Behind those closed doors, what fun might exist?

So here's to the laughter, to pranks and to schemes,
To the goofy memories that fuel funny dreams.
In shadows we gather, to chortle and cry,
For behind every door, there's a laugh waiting nigh!